MW01205119

SHORTER
ROAD
TO
SUCCESS

Linda Nash

Prism Publications   *St. Louis, Missouri*

THE SHORTER ROAD TO SUCCESS

Printed in the United States of America.
Cover design by Meinecke/Kemper Design
Page Design and Layout by Bill Farnsworth

ISBN: 0-9636702-1-2
Library of Congress Number 96-92278

Published by:
Prism Publications
P.O. Box 16873
St. Louis, Missouri 63105
314 725-9782

Dedication

To my daughters, Erika and Adrienne.

THE
SHORTER ROAD
TO
SUCCESS

Introduction

The frightening curves, dangerous drop-offs and unexpected hazards on the long road to success cause many to give up and find a comfortable parking place. For those willing to press on and overcome the obstacles, the rewards are great.

This is a guide book filled with short tips gleaned from both my personal and professional experience and many who have traveled the road before. Apply them to your own journey. You will shorten the trip and avoid some of the more treacherous potholes and curves.

What is success? That is yours to choose. Some say money, good health, wonderful relationships or fame. My favorite definition comes from Christopher Morley who said, "There is only one success, to be able to spend your life in your own way." It is your life. Enjoy the journey.

ATTITUDE

EXPECTATIONS

RESPONSIBILITY

Your attitude is your
life jacket in life.
It will keep you afloat.

Your attitude is your choice.

Choose to look for the positive possibilities in every situation and you will increase your opportunities for success.

A positive attitude is the
hallmark of successful people.

**Negativity is a contagious
disease, and it can become chronic.
Stay away from people who say
"you can't do that; you're not smart enough,
pretty enough, educated enough, etc."
These people are frequently
relatives or so called friends.**

Avoid them.

**Misery loves company.
Don't join.**

Surround yourself with positive, successful people. They might offer constructive criticism. If you pay attention, though, they will help you grow and become successful, too.

Your relationships and
your work are the only
things of real value in life.
Make them meaningful.

Each day is a new opportunity
to move forward with your life.
Let go of the past, it is over.
Concentrate on the now.

Live your life fully aware.
Suffer the pain, celebrate the
joy and cherish the moment.
Living is an activity.
Do it.

Be enthusiastic.
Live with passion.

We create prisons for ourselves
from other peoples expectations.
Don't live someone else's dream.

Shoulds and oughts are red flags. Evaluate them. If they're a guilt trip based on someone else's values and expectations, eliminate them.

You will always live up to your expectations, however high or low, good or bad they may be.

If you expect to be mediocre,
you can count on it.

Expect the best.

Wanting something is not the same as expecting to get it.

**Expecting is believing.
Believers make things happen.**

BELIEVE IN YOURSELF.
If you don't believe in yourself,
don't expect others to believe in
you either.

Get *can't* out of your vocabulary.

Discipline yourself.
Avoid the excuse,
"I'll do it as soon as ..."

Do the most
important things first.
Don't rationalize.
Prioritize.

**Success always exacts a price
which must be paid up front.
If you are unwilling to pay,
don't expect to achieve.**

Like goldfish, people tend to grow only as much as the container in which they live. Make sure your container is expandable.

You are limited only by what you believe you can do, and your willingness to do it.

Never apologize for
who or what you are.
What is, is.
Accept it and move
forward from there.

Life is a series of obstacles
designed to help you grow. Whether
you grow or not is up to you.

Fear can keep you from
achieving your dreams.
If you don't face the fear,
you will always wonder what
might have been. Don't wonder.

Failure is but a lesson to be learned.
Learn from it and move on.

Blaming your parents, your teachers or your company is a waste of your valuable time.
It produces nothing.
Get busy doing what you need to do to make your life happen!

You become what you think
about most. Well ... ?

It's your life.
Plan it.
Manage it.
Live it!

Be the best that you can
at whatever you do.
If you don't you
will disappoint yourself.

LEARNING AND EDUCATION

**Dedicate yourself to
life long learning.**

Learn something new every day.

Learn something from
everyone you meet.
We are all teachers.
Some of the most valuable
lessons in life come
from unlikely sources.

Read books and magazines.

Listen to
educational/motivational tapes.

Stay informed.
Know what is happening in
the world and your profession.
Don't allow yourself
to become obsolete.

Take a course to learn or
improve a skill.

Take a course for fun.
Fun counts, too.

Keep up with technology.
Don't make excuses.
The pace is fast but you can do it.
Don't be left behind.

Make friends with your librarian.
Librarians know how to find any
information you may need.
And, it's free! Just ask.

Learn a new language if
you know only one.
If you know two, learn three.
Technology has removed
time and distance barriers.
We must understand each other to
function in a global environment.

Learn everything you can.

Keep growing.

Don't stagnate.

Opportunities are endless
if you are prepared.

Career and Work

Your career belongs to you.
Manage it. If you give control of
it to a company or another
individual, don't blame them
when things go wrong.

Do what you love.
If you love what you do,
everyday is a joy.

A job is something you do to make money. Your work is something you do for fulfillment. Work is more fun, and you can even make money doing it.

Market yourself, your skills, your ideas to:

- your boss

- a prospective boss

- your customers

Everyone is your customer.
Your boss, your coworkers, your
employees and yes, the people we
usually call customers.

Provide incredible
customer service.
Exceed expectations.

Know your customers.

Know their names, birthdays,
education, hobbies, everything!

Building relationships
builds success.

People like to help, work with and buy from people they know.

Deliver what you promise.
Over deliver!

You'll be remembered.

Stand up straight.

Shoulders back, chin up.

Walk with confidence.

You'll look important.

Manicure your nails. Men, too.

Polish your shoes.

Dress a little better than your job calls for.

Better yet, dress for the position you want.

Don't ever say, "It's not my job."

Always follow up.

Be punctual.

Start meetings on time.

Stay on time.

Perform your work as if you own the company.

If you owned the company would you hire you?

Go the extra mile.
Then go a little further.

Explore new solutions.

Be creative.

Be innovative.

Look at things sideways.

Find a better way.

Change the way entirely.

Don't get stuck
in a dead end job.
Move.

Complacency means you'll
stay in the same place.
You can do that in quicksand.

Find a mentor. Whether you are beginning a new profession or life direction or have already moved down the path a good distance, learn from the best.

Get honest feedback from those
you respect.

Make changes. Keep improving.

Doing a good job is not enough. Take on new assignments, learn new skills, keep growing.

Make yourself valuable.

Become an expert.
Experts are valued.

Perception is reality.
If your professional image
needs to be changed, do it.

Once you learn a job well, you probably need to move up or out.

Staying too long in the same position will put you at risk. Salary increases and promotions will be based on attitude, skill level and value to the company, not longevity.

If you are fired, downsized, merged or re-engineered out of a job, don't burn bridges. Pain and anger are understandable but don't act on them. You need all the bridges you can find in life.

Interviewing for a new position
when you are angry with
your last boss or company
is usually self defeating.
Would you hire an angry person?
Get over it and move on.

Networking is the best way to
find a new job.
Maintain and constantly expand
your network.

Join professional organizations.
Be active.

Chair committees and events.

Learn to lead.

Write articles for
newspapers or newsletters.

If you can't write, learn.

Improve your presentation skills.

Never be a bore.

Learn how to make the
boring interesting.

Make the interesting exciting.

Never call others work your own.
Be original.
There's only one you.

Write down your great ideas
immediately. They might
be lost forever if you don't.

Be an initiator.
Ask for new opportunities.

Be a participant.
Watching from the sidelines
could keep you out of the game.

Develop your leadership skills.

Remember that true
leaders have followers.
Willing ones!

Never be mediocre!
Strive to be the best.

If you're not successful yet,
act like it.

HEALTH AND WELLNESS

Take care of your body.

Exercise. Eat reasonably.

Get regular medical checkups.

Exercise makes you feel better, look better, perform better. It doesn't have to feel like punishment. Take a walk, go dancing, or play ball with your children. Just keep moving.

If your belt buckle faces the floor, you're either standing over a powerful magnet or you need to make changes in your lifestyle.

Smile a lot, even when
you don't feel like it.

Feeling often follows action.

At the end of every day, think of at least one positive thing that occurred. On some days this takes longer than others, but you'll find something.

Keep balance in your life.
Workaholics are rarely happy.

To the extent you take control of your life, you reduce your stress. Let go of the things you can't control, however painful. Take control of what you can.

Laugh a lot. It's good for you.

Learn to laugh at yourself.

INTERPERSONAL

Become a good communicator.
It's crucial!

Listening is the most important
communication skill.

Listen more.
Really listen.
Your success may depend on it.

Ask

for

help, advice, support, direction, clarification, information, resources, or anything else you need.

Be sure to ask qualified people.

Validate other peoples
feelings and point of view.
You might disagree
but don't devalue.

Become a "win-win" negotiator.
Contrary to most of the
games we play, there doesn't
always have to be a loser.

Enjoy your family and friends.

Be a role model for your children.
What you do is more important
than what you say.

Volunteer.
Giving is receiving.

Give of your time, energy, knowledge, ability, and if you have it, money, to a worthy cause.

Be a friend. Offer help, advice or
support when needed.
A batch of cookies is great, too.

Say "THANK YOU."
Do it in writing.
The written word makes it real.

Praise generously when it is due and do it publicly. A "pat on the back" means a lot. Having it said in public multiplies it by the number of people who hear it or read it.

NETWORK

NETWORK

NETWORK

Meet new people wherever you go.

Sometimes you need to speak first.

Shake hands and smile.

Show interest in other people
and they will be more likely
to show interest in you.

Sit with new people at meetings.

Get business cards from the
people you meet.
Make notes on the back so you
don't forget why you have the card.

Value everyone.

Treat all people as if
they're important.
They are.

Let people know what
you expect of them.

Know what people expect of you.
If you don't know, ask.

Functioning without focus
produces random results.

It also produces misunderstanding,
conflict and hurt feelings.

Resolve conflicts.
Good communication skills help.

Give others the opportunity to succeed.

Good manners are
never out of style.
Use them.

Be courteous to secretaries and receptionists. They deserve your respect, and, don't forget, they are the gatekeepers.

Treat everyone with respect.

Remember birthdays.
Write them on your calendar.
Send a card.

Send congratulatory notes for promotions, new jobs, articles published, awards won or any new achievement.

Call your mother just to say hello.

Even better, take her to lunch.

That goes for dads, sisters, brothers, or friends, too.

Give someone you care
about flowers.
One is OK.

Appreciate differences.

Value and understand other cultures.

SPIRITUALITY

Meditate, pray or spend some
quiet time alone each day.
If you are extremely busy
spend even more.

Silence is a precious commodity
that is difficult to find in a
chaotic world.
It is only in silence that you
can find the real you.

Each of us has a purpose,
a reason for being.
Why are you here?
What is your mission?
Put it in writing, and read it daily.

You are free to the extent that you
believe you can control what
happens in your life.
To the extent you do not believe,
you are enslaved.

Worry represents increased
stress and wasted time.
It has no value.

Learn to visualize.
See yourself as you want to be.
See every detail and action.
Believe.

Look for the potential for
good in all people, things,
and circumstances.

Goodness, like beauty,
is in the eye of the beholder.
We will find goodness if
we look for it, and often in the
measure we seek it.

Anonymous

What you love in other people is
what you love in yourself.
What you despise in other people
is what you despise in yourself.
Look into your own mirror
before judging others.

Assisting other people in
reaching their goals will
help you in reaching yours.

Give everyone you meet a gift,
even if it is just a smile.

**Appreciate the small things.
Each is a gift.**

Remember little kindnesses.

Enjoy who you are.
You are unique.

Happiness comes from within.
It cannot be provided by other
people or things.

Forgive yourself.

Focus on the good in yourself.
Help it grow.

Enjoy the natural
beauty around you.
The world is a wondrous place.
Every season has its glory.

Look for beauty everywhere.

The most evident token and
apparent sign of true wisdom
is a constant and
unconstrained rejoicing.

Montaigne

FINANCE AND MONEY

Control your finances.
If your house, your car, or your
credit card payments seem to
own you instead of you them,
you're in trouble.

Evaluate your net worth every year.
It's a way of keeping score.

SAVE

Begin when you're young.
If you're not young
begin now and save more.
How much are you
spending on nothing?

Invest carefully.
If it sounds too good to be true ...
well, you know the rest.

Spend on things of value.
Things of value usually last.
People do, houses do,
educations do, great paintings do,
but cars don't.
OK, classic cars, maybe.

Spend just for fun occasionally.

GOALS

Set goals and make a plan.

Put your plan in writing.

Set a timeline for your plan.

Do it.

Goals are worthless if they sit in a drawer gathering dust. You must take action. Divide the goal into achievable parts, set reasonable deadlines and meet them.
A deadline is your alarm clock. If you miss it, you will be late for the next goal.

Plan for your future.
Where do you want to be in
five years, 10 years, or 20 years?

Give yourself options.

Explore your options.

You can always detour along the way.

Commit to your goals.

Once you truly commit,
the help you need will appear.

Be sure you're watching for it.

Be sure you act on it.

CHANGE AND OTHER MUSINGS

CHANGE IS A CATALYST, NOT A CATASTROPHE.

Change will get you
"off the dime."

Change will make you reevaluate.

Change will help propel you
to a new and exciting future.

Embrace it.

Change presents many
exciting opportunities.
Stay alert.

Spend less time asking why and more time asking how.

Be flexible.
If you can stay with the flow you
won't be lost in the flood.

Approach all problems
as opportunities. Ask yourself,
"what can I learn from this?"

Never give up.
Persevere.

Listen to your head and your heart but follow your gut.

The road to success is
dotted with many
tempting parking places.

Don't park!

Keep dreaming new dreams.
Always have new goals.
Live life to the fullest.
Enjoy the journey.

This Is My Life

I promise that I will take charge of the
  direction and quality of my life.
I alone am responsible for me and my
  actions or inaction.
I will not blame others for my failures nor
  will I allow others to take credit for my
  successes.
I will work diligently to constantly improve
  who I am and what I am.
I will be proud of every accomplishment,
  however small.

And, I will remind others to be proud, too.

I will recognize that each step brings me closer to my goals. Each failure is but a lesson to be learned.

I will be courageous and face my fears knowing that in doing so my strength will double.

I will realize my dreams, one by one. And, I will support others in their dreams.

This is my life. I will live it to the fullest.

Linda Nash

Linda Nash is a nationally known speaker, consultant, seminar leader and author. An MBA with more than 20 years of hands-on experience, she has been a journalist, producer in radio, corporate VP, entrepreneur and mom. She knows what works and what doesn't .

Known for the unexpected, Linda shares her expertise and unique insights in the areas of Success, Change, Communication, Team Building and Personal Growth. She is a member of the National Speakers Association and past president of the St. Louis Gateway Chapter.

Linda's combination of immediately applicable techniques coupled with her enthusiasm, dry wit, great stories and motivational style inspire her audiences to enjoy life's journey and succeed every day.

For more information on
Linda's books, tapes, speeches,
seminars or consulting services contact:

L.J. Nash and Associates, Inc.
P.O. Box 16873
St. Louis, MO. 63105
314-725-9782